Contents

Books in Series

A Natural Beautiful You

Want to learn about African Magic, Wicca, or even Reiki while cleaning your home, exercising, or driving to work? I know it's tough these days to simply find the time to relax and curl up with a good book. This is why I'm delighted to share that I have books available in audiobook format.

Best of all, you can get the audiobook version of this book or any other book by me for free as part of a 30-day Audible trial.

Members get free audiobooks every month and exclusive discounts. It's an excellent way to explore and determine if audiobook learning works for you.

If you're not satisfied, you can cancel anytime within the

trial period. You won't be charged, and you can still keep your book. To choose your free audiobook, visit:

www.mojosiedlak.com/free-audiobooks

WANT TO BE FIRST TO KNOW?!

JOIN MY NEWSLETTER!
MOJOSIEDLAK.COM/SELF-HELP-AND-YOGA-NEWSLETTER

Introduction

Your skin goes through a process of naturally shedding older, dead skin cells and replaces them with new cells once every 3o days or so. Sometimes though, these older cells don't dislodge naturally. That can lead to patches of dry and flaky skin or clogged pores. Just like you would exfoliate your face, the rest of your body could also benefit from exfoliation. A body scrub is a physical exfoliant that mechanically scrubs dead skin cells off your skin. A body scrub aims to remove the dead skin cells and encourage the healthy production of new ones.

ONE

Benefits of Body Scrubs

Improve Skin Texture and Color

THERE ARE SEVERAL BENEFITS TO USING A BODY SCRUB. THE top of the list is smoother, softer skin texture. If you have patches of dry, flaky, or itchy skin, body scrub can go a long way to help remove the dead skin cells and reveal softer, fresher skin beneath it.

Darker areas of skin can happen for several reasons. Age, pregnancy, and overall changes in your hormonal balances can often lead to darker skin patches forming. Exfoliating with a body scrub can help break up the dark pigmentation, encouraging the darker area to fade.

Preventing Ingrown Hairs and Body Acne

When you wax, you remove the hair, root and all. The hair grows back, but it is weaker than before and may not be able to push through the skin. The trapped hair causes a red, sometimes itchy bump to form called an ingrown hair. Exfoliating the area will remove the dead skin and allow the hair to emerge more easily, preventing the chances of ingrown hairs.

Body acne has two common causes. Friction between your skin and your clothing causes the lining of your skin pores to break down. The top layer of skin cells dies while bacteria and your sweat get trapped, causing a breakout. The second cause is your skin getting clogged with excess sebum and dead skin cells, causing hair follicles to become inflamed. Regular exfoliation with a body scrub can help prevent the build-up of dead skin cells, lowering the chances of trapped sweat, bacteria, and dirt, reducing body acne risk.

Detoxification and Cellulite Control

The action of rubbing and massaging the exfoliant over your skin will boost blood circulation to the skin surface and help drain your lymph nodes. All that improved circulation will help draw out impurities from your body. Body scrubs can form a part of a detoxification process.

The increase in circulation will also help your body get rid of cellulite, small pockets of fat under the skin.

Better Skincare Product Absorption

Dead skin cells sitting on the surface of your skin can prevent your skincare products from penetrating and being absorbed. Your moisturizers will be far less effective, causing a potential lack of hydration, which in turn can lead up to the build-up of even more dead skin cells. Exfoliating with a body scrub will prevent dead skin cells' build-up, allowing the moisturizer and any other skincare products to be easily absorbed.

Improve Skin Elasticity

Regular long-term exfoliation can increase your skin's collagen production. Collagen is a major component of the skin's connectivity, providing structure and preventing lines and wrinkles. As we age, our body's natural ability to produce collagen decreases. Using a body scrub regularly can help stimulate your skin's collagen production, promoting skin elasticity, and minimizing sagging.

TWO

Components of a Body Scrub

THE MAIN COMPONENT OF ANY BODY SCRUB IS THE GRANULES that perform the mechanical exfoliation or scrubbing. This chapter will introduce three types of scrubs that you can use when you create your DIY body scrub at home.

Sugar Scrub Benefits

Sugar is a gentler exfoliator than salt, as its granules are rounder and, therefore, less abrasive. Sugar is a glycolic acid source, also known as alpha-hydroxy acids (AHA), which breaks down the layers of dead skin cells. It also helps speed up the skin's rehydration. Sugar scrub is a good option if you are prone to dry skin. Sugar scrubs are also a good choice for more sensitive skin, or older, more mature skin because of it's gentler properties.

Types of Sugars

There are three types of sugars you can use for DIY body scrubs. All of these sugars come from the sugarcane plant, also known as the sugar beet. The difference is in the way they are processed and refined. The juice containing the sugar is extracted from the plant. The sugary juice is purified and heated to form molasses, which is a concentrated, sugary syrup. The sugar crystals are separated from the molasses in a machine called a centrifuge that spins very fast. White sugar is then processed to remove any excess molasses, giving it a white color. The crystals are also smaller.

Brown sugar is white sugar that has had some of the molasses added back. Turbinado sugar is the product produced from the centrifuge, and its crystals are larger than the other kinds. You may need to experiment to see which type of sugar works best for your skin.

White sugar is compatible with most skin types and carries the benefits mentioned in the chapter's start.

Brown sugar has some molasses added to it. The molasses contains some vitamins and minerals that could benefit your skin. Its crystals are, however, not as large as turbinado sugar, making it a gentler option.

Turbinado sugar is the least refined sugar. It has more molasses in its composition than brown sugar. Its crystals are larger and, therefore, more abrasive than the other two. If you have extremely delicate skin, you may find turbinado too rough.

Sea Salt Scrub Benefits

Salt has bigger crystals with sharper edges than sugar. These properties make it particularly useful for areas with thicker, rough skin, such as the elbows and feet. Sea salt has natural trace minerals, which are natural purifiers. They draw out pore-clogging toxins, invigorating your skin, and promoting circulation.

A salt scrub is suitable for oilier skin types, as it will help decongest your skin. If you have dry skin, be aware that salt can dry out your skin more. If your skin is very thin or sensitive, salt may be too coarse and irritate your skin.

Types of Salt

Finely ground sea salt is less coarse than the regular sea salt and is an alternative if you find the larger sea salt crystals too abrasive. It is not really a type of salt. It is merely a type of grind. Finely ground sea salt might be better suited to larger areas or areas that get red quickly.

Epsom salt is high in magnesium and famed for their muscle relaxing properties. These salts are excellent for use on elbows and feet. It can also assist in the control of psoriasis or eczema.

Himalayan pink salt is commonly available. It is considered one of the purest salts on earth and is said to have anti-inflammatory properties. Himalayan pink salts are usually one of the most coarse salts available, meaning the granules are very large.

Hawaiian salt, also known as black lava salt, gets its color from the activated charcoal contained in it. Activated charcoal is very effective at drawing out toxins. Hawaiian salt may also help reduce water retention and ease muscle cramps.

If you find a salt you want to use but find it too coarse and harsh on your skin, consider using a coffee grinder to grind the salt down. Grinding the salt will make it finer and less abrasive on your skin.

Coffee Scrub Benefits

Coffee scrubs make use of coffee grounds. You can make use of fresh coffee grounds or used coffee grounds. Most people prefer to use used coffee grounds. It is a way to recycle what would otherwise essentially be seen as waste and thrown out. Coffee grounds contain caffeine, and caffeine is known to have antioxidants. The benefits of antioxidants for skin are quite well known. Antioxidants help combat free radicals, such as those from UV light and protect healthy skin cells. This effect helps fight the photoaging effect of sunlight on your skin. Caffeine is also known for helping fight cellulite as it prevents excessive fat from building up in skin cells. It also increases circulation in the small blood vessels on the surface of your skin, encouraging new skin cell growth.

Coffee grounds also contain Vitamin B3, which can help prevent skin growths and some nonmelanoma skin cancers. Coffee scrub is also excellent for helping reduce pigmentation in dark patches of skin. It has an overall skin lightening effect.

Types of Coffee Grounds

There are as many types of coffee grounds as there is coffee. The best recommendation here is to experiment and find what kind of coffee blend works best with your skin type.

Keep in mind coffee grounds can be hard and very abrasive, especially when compared to sugar. Coffee grounds do have the bonus of smelling like your favorite morning pick-me-up beverage.

THREE

Moisturizing Choices

WHEN CREATING YOUR BODY SCRUB AT HOME, YOU NEED A moisturizing base oil. This oil will help the salt, sugar, or coffee grounds clump together and be easier to apply to your skin. The moisturizing oil will also help to nourish your skin during the exfoliation process. This chapter will introduce four popular oils often used as moisturizing choices when creating your DIY body scrub and their different benefits.

Coconut Oil

Coconut oil helps lock moisture into your skin. It also increases the skin's barrier function, which helps protect your skin against outside stressors, such as the sun's harmful UV rays. Coconut oil restores the skin's natural pH levels helping you get that silky smooth finish. The lauric acid found in coconut oil has antimicrobial properties that can help reduce any skin inflammation. Coconut oil also contains antioxidants, making it great for combating skin aging.

Using coconut oil as a base can help reduce any irritation your skin might experience from exfoliation's mechanical action. It makes a good choice if you have sensitive skin. If you are prone to body acne, you may want to avoid coconut oil as it is heavy and may clog your pores, aggravating acne breakouts.

Jojoba Oil

Jojoba oil is pronounced ho-ho-ba oil and is an oil extracted from the seeds of the jojoba plant. Its oil most closely resembles the oil produced by the human skin making it easily absorbed. This property also makes it suitable for use on all skin types. Jojoba oil will help moisturize dry skin and balance oily skin. Jojoba oil is an excellent choice for a moisturizing base for your body scrub.

Jojoba oil contains antioxidants that help combat skin aging. It also helps improve skin elasticity and reduces fine lines. It is rich in Vitamins A, D, and E. These vitamins are amazing skin food that encourages skin cell regeneration. It also has anti-inflammatory and antimicrobial properties that will help control body acne, eczema, and psoriasis.

Grapeseed Oil

Grapeseed oil is extracted from the seeds of grapes after they are used for making wine. It is a light oil that is quickly absorbed by the skin. Unlike coconut oil, it does not tend to clog pores, so even those with oily skin can use it without worry.

Grapeseed oil has extremely powerful antioxidant properties thanks to the polyphenol compounds it contains. The compounds mean that grapeseed oil will help fight the signs of aging in the skin, including sunspots and wrinkles. Grapeseed oil also has a lot of vitamin E and omega fatty acids that help provide the skin with what it needs to stay healthy.

Grapeseed oil is known for its anti-inflammatory and antimicrobial properties. It helps to cleanse the skin deeply and prevent breakouts. It will also lessen any skin redness. Grapeseed oil can also help even out your skin tone and alleviate any dark marks or spots you may have. As a bonus, grapeseed oil can lighten scars.

Sweet Almond Oil

Sweet almond oil is made from the sweet almond or Prunus amygdalus var. dulcis. If you have a nut allergy, steer clear of this oil.

Sweet almond oil is good for hydration of the skin. It is well known in ancient China, Ayurvedic, and Greco-Persian cultures for its treatment of dry skin and its ability to reduce scar appearance.

Sweet almond oil is packed with several skin-nourishing nutrients such as vitamin A, vitamin E, omega-3 fatty acids, and zinc. This oil has antioxidant properties and helps fight premature skin aging. Sweet almond oil can also help protect your skin against UV rays from the sun. It has anti-inflammatory properties that can help soothe skin irritation.

Sweet almond oil is known to help prevent stretch marks. It also reduces dark blotches or patches and improves your skin's complexion over time.

Choosing Your Moisturizing Oil

When choosing a moisturizing oil for your skin, be sure to read the label. Look for organic oil, meaning it has been grown without the use of pesticides. Virgin means it has been made from fresh plants. Non-hydrogenated oil is best, as the hydrogenation process can create trans fats, which are best avoided.

Cold-pressed or expeller-pressed oil is what you want. Cold-pressed means there was no heat or chemicals used in the extraction process. Heat and chemicals can change the chemical nature of the oil.

Avoid any **RBD** oils, as they have been bleached and deodorized, not something you want on your skin. These extra processes can remove many of the nutrients and antioxidants in the oil, making it less beneficial.

Look for seals of approval, such as "Fairtrade Certified," meaning the oil has been ethically sourced. And a "Non-GMO Seal of Approval," meaning the oil has not been genetically modified.

FOUR

Essential Oils

WHILE SUGAR, SALT, OR COFFEE GRANULES AND A moisturizing base form the two main components of your DIY body scrub, you can also consider adding some extra in the form of essential oils. There is a wide variety of essential oils that you can add to your body scrub. In this chapter, we will explore a few of the options available and their benefits. Some common oils are:

Lavender Oil

By far, one of the most popular essential oils, lavender oil, has many positive effects. Lavender oil is made from the lavender plant, Lavandula angustifolia, originally from France. It has antioxidant properties that help protect your skin from environmental stressors. Lavender oil has antibacterial and fungicidal effects that will help protect your skin against infection. It can also help reduce dark spots or skin discoloration. Lavender oil can also help relax your muscles and ease menstrual pains. A bonus, lavender oil can ward off those pesky bug bites.

Aside from its effect from the skin application, lavender

oil's aroma is said to have positive results. It can help with insomnia, anxiety, and is a general mood uplifter. Using a scrub with lavender oil at night before bed could help you get a great night's sleep.

Peppermint Oil

Peppermint has been used for its medicinal properties since ancient times. Records of the use of peppermint can be traced back as far as ancient Egypt. Peppermint oil is made from the plant Mentha piperita. It is known for its ability to cleanse and rejuvenate the skin. If your skin seems dull, adding peppermint oil to your body scrub can restore your skin's natural glow. It is one of the many essential oils that have antibacterial properties to help protect your skin. Peppermint oil is also a great choice to soothe dry and itchy skin.

As much as humans enjoy the scent of peppermint, bugs hate it, making it a good insect repellent. The aroma of peppermint oil is said to help with respiration issues. If you have a slight cold or your sinuses feel stuffy, a body scrub with peppermint oil can help ease those problems. It can also reduce stress and reduce the pain from headaches. Peppermint oil aroma can give you a mental boost, not to mention it will leave you smelling fresh and cool.

Sweet Orange Oil

Sweet orange oil is made from the peel or rind of the sweet orange, Citrus sinensis. It has antimicrobial and antifungal properties that help protect your skin against infections and breakouts. Sweet orange oil contains limonene, a strong antioxidant that will protect your skin against environmental factors such as pollution and UV rays. Sweet orange oil is packed with vitamin C, great for nourishing your skin.

The aroma of sweet orange oil also has beneficial properties. It can help reduce pain, decrease stress, and uplift your overall mood. It is also said to give you a nice mental boost. Using a scrub with sweet orange oil in the mornings could help start your day off just right.

Rose Oil

Roses aren't just pretty smelling flowers. They have wonderful properties when their petals are distilled into rose essential oil. Rose oil is made from the petals of Rosa damascena.

Rose oil gently hydrates your skin. It has antifungal and antibacterial properties that help cleanse your skin and prevent breakouts. It reduces the signs of aging and can even lighten the appearance of scars. Rose oil can help ease muscle cramps and pains, including menstrual discomfort.

The aroma of rose oil has its own set of benefits, such as reducing stress and anxiety. It can also help ease some depressive symptoms.

Oils That Irritate Skin

Do not use undiluted essential oils directly on your skin. The oils are very concentrated and can be prone to irritating the skin or causing skin sensitization. You only need a drop or two in your DIY scrub to get their benefits.

Any essential oil has the potential to irritate your skin. For this reason, you should always do a patch test on a small part of your skin before using it over a large portion of your body. However, some essential oils are known to be more likely to irritate your skin than others. Below is a list of oils that, even if diluted, may still cause skin irritation. This list is by no means complete. Also, keep in mind that each person's skin is different, and you may find your skin reacting badly to oils that are not on this list.

Allspice

Bay Laurel
Cassia
Catnip
Cinnamon (Bark and Leaves)
Clove
Lemongrass
Litsea Cubeba (May Chang)
Melissa
Oakmoss
Oregano
Parsley
Peru Balsam
Sage
Thyme

Oils to Avoid in Pregnancy

The number one rule here is always to consult your qualified healthcare provider or doctor, especially if you are uncertain about anything. You should avoid using essential oils in your scrub during the first trimester of pregnancy. The first trimester is the most critical period of your pregnancy. It is best to avoid exposing yourself and your baby to a potentially toxic substance. If you wish to add essential oil to your DIY body scrub during the second and third trimester, dilution is key. Consider halving the amount you would typically use in your recipe.

Many essential oils have not been tested for their safety during pregnancy. Below is a list of essential oils you will want to steer clear of. The list is by no means complete, so again, always consult with your healthcare provider.

Aniseed
Arnica
Basil
Birch

Bitter almond
Boldo leaf
Broom
Buchu
Calamus
Camphor (brown or yellow)
Cassia
Cedarwood/thuja
Chervil
Cinnamon
Clary sage
Clove (bud, leaf or stem)
Coriander
Costus
Elecampane
Fennel
Horseradish
Hyssop
Jaborandi leaf
Juniper berry
Melilotus
Mugwort
Mustard
Nutmeg
Oak Mass
Origanum
Parsley
Pennyroyal
Pine
Rosemary
Rue
Sage
Sassafras
Savin
Savory

Tansy
Tarragon
Thyme
Tonka
Wintergreen
Wormwood

Additional Warnings

Essential oils can and do expire. The shelf life of essential oil depends on the type of oil. You can increase your oil's shelf life by storing it in a dark place away from heat. Do some research on the quality of a brand before buying.

As much as you might love a particular essential oil, keep in mind, what is right for you may not be suitable for your pet. Some essential oils are toxic to dogs and cats. Be sure to keep your body scrub and essential oils well out of reach of pets and children.

FIVE

Mixing Your Body Scrub

A BODY SCRUB HAS TWO BASIC INGREDIENTS: THE EXFOLIANT granules and moisturizing oil that loosely bind those granules together. You don't need to add anything else, but a few drops of essential oils will allow you to customize your DIY scrub a little further.

In this chapter, we will review the basic formula for putting together a DIY body scrub at home, as well as how you can modify it to make it your very own.

The Mix

In chapter two, we reviewed three exfoliant granule types: sugar, salt, and coffee. Chapter 3 covered moisturizing options. By now, you probably already have an idea of which ones you would like to try.

Most body scrubs follow the ratio of exfoliant 2 to moisturizer 1. For example, if you are making a sugar scrub with sweet almond oil, you will use two cups of sugar with one sweet almond oil cup. Of course, if you want to make only one scrub cup, you need to use half a cup of moisturizing oil.

You can adjust the ratio as you feel needed to what best

suits your skin. You can also try a combination of different exfoliating granules together, for example, salt and sugar.

Once you have mixed your basic scrub, you can add in the essential oil. A few drops will be more than enough. Keep the size of the batch you are making in mind. Around five or so drops per cup of exfoliant should be enough.

With this basic formula in mind, the combinations of body scrubs you can create at home is almost limitless. However, if you feel a bit overwhelmed and want a place to start, you could always try out one of the recipes below.

Keep these items handy when you want to whip up a batch of body scrub:

- Mixing Bowl
- Measuring Cups (Or Spoons)
- Spoons For Mixing
- A Sealable Jar Or Container To Store The Scrub In

DIY Body Scrub Recipes

Fight the Cellulite
Body scrub to help tighten and tone your skin while loosening the excess fat cells stored there.

- 1 cup coffee grounds
- 1/2 a cup of coconut oil
- 5 drops of peppermint essential oil

Relaxing Night Scrub
Pamper yourself after a long day with this relaxing scrub. Rejuvenate your skin and help yourself get a good night's rest.

- 1 cup of sugar
- 1/2 a cup of jojoba oil

- 5 drops of lavender essential oil

Zesty Morning Scrub

Start your day off with an energy-boosting body scrub. This scrub will give your skin and mood a boost to face the day.

- 1 cup of salt
- 1/2 a cup Grapeseed oil
- 5 drops of sweet orange essential oil

Switch It Up

The recipes mentioned above only make use of one essential oil each. Nothing is stopping you from experimenting by adding two or three different essential oils. For example, you could add three drops of sweet orange essential oil and two drops of peppermint essential oil to the zesty morning scrub instead of just sweet orange essential oil. You can also add a few more drops of essential oil if you wish, but don't overdo it, as essential oils are very concentrated. Experiment and see what works for you and what you like best.

Shelf Life

The shelf life of your DIY body scrub will largely depend on what type of exfoliant granules you used. Coffee grounds may only last a week or two at most. Sugar and salt scrubs will last a bit longer, up to around six months. Use an airtight, water-tight jar to store your body scrub. The most crucial tip to extending your body scrub's shelf life is to keep the container or jar closed as much as possible.

If you plan on using a jar, select one with stainless steel fasteners and flip lid. Mason jars with a twist top lid may rust over time. Sterilize your jars or containers and your mixing tools when creating your scrub to help prevent any contamination. Create a small batch of body scrub so that you can use all of it before it is likely to go off. Use common sense—if your body scrub looks off or smells strange, it is best to discard it and mix a new batch.

SIX

How to Use a Body Scrub

BODY SCRUBS CAN BECOME A PART OF YOUR REGULAR BATH OR shower routine. Over exfoliation will damage your skin, so only use a body scrub once or twice a week. As with all skin products, you should test your reaction to the scrub on a small patch of skin first, the day before. This way, you can see if you have any adverse reactions to the ingredients before applying it all over yourself.

Bath Body Scrub

If you plan to use your body scrub in conjunction with a bath, here is how to go about it. Run yourself a bath. Make sure the water is not too hot. A luke-warm to warm temperature is what you are after. Soak your body in the water for a while. Warm water will help open up your skin's pores and make it more susceptible to deep cleaning. Soak in the bath for around 10 minutes, if possible. Once done soaking, you can either stand in the bathtub or if you are uncomfortable doing so, climb out of the tub.

Apply the scrub using your hands. Use circular motions to exfoliate your skin. Start at your feet and work your way upwards to your heart. Once you have completed exfoliating yourself with the scrub, it's time to get back into the bathtub. Rinse off the body scrub from your skin. You don't want any of those particles left behind as they may irritate your skin, especially when there is friction between them, your skin, and your clothing.

Shower Body Scrub

The process of using a body scrub in the shower is very similar to using one in the bath. First, you will want to run the shower and soak in luke-warm to warm water to open your skin's pores. Stand and soak for around 10 minutes. Then shut off the water and begin to apply your body scrub. Start from your feet and work your way upwards in circular motions towards your heart. Once you have completed the exfoliation process, you can turn on the water and rinse the scrub off. Be sure there are no particles left behind.

Things to Keep in Mind

Soap Before or After?

The debate on whether it is better to wash your body with soap before you exfoliate or after is sometimes hotly debated. Suppose you wash your body with soap before you exfoliate. In that case, you remove the dirt and sweat from your skin's surface, giving you a clean base from which to exfoliate the dead skin cells off with the body scrub. On the other hand, if you use a body scrub before washing with soap, you wash away the dirt, sweat, dead skin cells, and leftover scrub all at the same time. So which method is better? It's honestly up to personal preference. Experiment and find which works better for you.

How Much Pressure?

It is tempting to believe the harder you scrub, the more

you will benefit. However, if you feel any pain while exfoliating your skin, you are using too much pressure. Experiencing pain is an indication that you may be damaging healthy skin cells. Ease up on the pressure you are using while scrubbing.

Body Scrub Before or After Shaving?

If you are planning to shave, it's best to exfoliate right before you do. The body scrub will help remove the dead skin cells, potentially clogging your hair follicles or even trapping them. By preparing your skin for shaving with exfoliation, you will ensure a much closer shave. Give your skin some time to rest after shaving, two or three days, before your next body scrub application. Exfoliating then has the added benefit of reducing the chances of ingrown hairs.

Moisturizing

Using a body scrub and soap will strip your skin of its natural oils resulting in drier skin. It is a good idea to apply moisturizing lotion or oils to your skin after you have exfoliated with a body scrub. As you have removed all the dead skin cells, your skin will absorb them a lot more effectively. Sealing moisture into your skin will help you keep that fresh, softness longer after a body scrub exfoliation.

When Not to Use Body Scrub

If your skin is irritated, it is best not to use a body scrub. For example, if you have sunburn or a rash of some kind, stay clear of your body scrubbing routine for the time being. Using a body scrub can worsen the condition. Give your skin the time it needs to heal.

SEVEN

Sugar Scrub Recipes

You may find that after allowing your scrub to sit for a period of time, the sugar might settle down to the bottom. It may be necessary to shake your scrub up a little bit before using.

Peppermint Sugar Scrub

- 1 cup White Sugar
- ½ cup Your Choice of Carrier Oil
- 12 drops Peppermint Essential Oil

Orange Sugar Scrub

- 1 cup Brown Sugar
- ½ cup your Choice of Carrier Oil
- 12 drops Orange Essential Oil

Pumpkin Spice Vanilla Sugar Scrub

- 1 Cup White Sugar
- ½ cup your Choice of Carrier Oil
- ½ teaspoon Pure Vanilla Extract
- 5 drops Cinnamon Essential Oil
- 3 drops Clove Essential Oil
- 5 drops Ginger Essential Oil

Minty Cucumber Sugar Scrub

- 1 cup White Sugar
- ½ cup your Choice of Carrier Oil
- 6 drops Peppermint Essential Oil
- 6 drops Cucumber Essential Oil

Lavender and Vanilla Sugar Scrub

- 1 cup White Sugar
- ½ cup your Choice of Carrier Oil
- 8 drops Lavender Essential Oil
- 1 teaspoon Pure Vanilla Extract

Brown Sugar and Honey Scrub

- 1 cup Brown Sugar
- ¼ cup Olive Oil
- 12 drops Orange Essential Oil

Tranquility Sugar Scrub

- 1 cup White Sugar
- ½ cup Your Choice of Carrier Oil
- 6 drops Lavender Essential Oil
- 4 drops Vetiver Essential Oil
- 2 drops Sandalwood Essential Oil

Upbeat and Positive Sugar Scrub

- 1 cup White Sugar
- ½ cup your Choice of Carrier Oil
- 6 drops Wild Orange Essential Oil
- 4 drops Grapefruit Essential Oil
- 2 drops Spearmint Essential Oil

Mystical Rejuvenation Sugar Scrub

- 1 cup White Sugar
- ½ up your Choice of Carrier Oil
- 6 drops Frankincense Essential Oil
- 3 drops Cedar Wood Essential Oil
- 3 drops White Fir Essential Oil

Spring Breeze Sugar Scrub

- 1 cup White Sugar
- ½ cup your Choice of Carrier Oil
- 5 drops Rosemary Essential Oil
- 5 drops Lemon Essential Oil
- 2 drops Grapefruit Essential Oil

Energizing Sugar Scrub

- 1 cup White Sugar
- ½ cup your Choice of Carrier Oil
- 5 drops Grapefruit Essential Oil
- 5 drops Peppermint Essential Oil
- 2 drops Bergamot Essential Oil

Smooth and Silky Sugar Scrub

- 1 cup White Sugar
- ½ cup your Choice of Carrier Oil
- 6 drops Frankincense Essential Oil
- 6 drops Lavender Essential Oil

De-Stress Me Sugar Scrub

- 1 cup White Sugar
- ½ cup your Choice of Carrier Oil
- 6 drops Lavender Essential Oil
- 3 drops Lime Essential Oil
- 3 drops Mandarin Essential Oil

Fruity and Fun Sugar Scrub

- 1 cup White Sugar
- ½ cup your Choice of Carrier Oil
- 5 drops Mandarin Essential Oil
- 3 drops Neroli Essential Oil
- 2 drops Sweet Orange Essential Oil
- 2 drops Sandalwood Atlas Essential Oil

Orange Creamsicle Sugar Scrub

- 1 cup White Sugar
- ½ cup your Choice of Carrier Oil
- 8 drops Mandarin Orange Essential Oil
- 4 drops Vanilla Essential Oil

Moon Goddess Sugar Scrub

- 1 cup White Sugar
- ½ cup your Choice of Carrier Oil
- 6 drops Sandalwood Essential Oil
- 4 drops Lemon Essential Oil
- 2 drop Rose Essential Oil

Citrus Flower Sugar Scrub

- 1 cup white sugar
- ½ cup your choice of carrier oil
- 6 drops Frankincense Essential Oil
- 3 drops Lemongrass Essential Oil
- 3 drops Ylang Ylang Essential Oil

Simple Waters Sugar Scrub

- 1 cup White Sugar
- ½ cup your Choice of Carrier Oil
- 6 drops Patchouli Essential Oil
- 4 drops Frankincense Essential Oil
- 3 drops Grapefruit Essential Oil

EIGHT

Sea Salt Scrub Recipes

REMEMBER THAT THE FEEL OF YOUR SCRUB SHOULD NOT BE DRY and crumbling but then again it shouldn't be too oily and runny. You need to find that favorable middle between the two. Furthermore, you can always fine-tune any of these recipes to better suit your needs and preferences. If your scrub is too oily and runny simply add some additional sea salt. If your scrub is too dry, add some more oil.

Geranium Body Sea Salt Scrub

- 1 cup Fine Sea Salt
- ½ cup your Choice of Carrier Oil
- 15 drops Geranium Essential Oil

Coconut Rose Sea Salt Body Scrub

- 1 cup Fine Sea Salt
- 1/2 your softened Coconut Oil
- 15 drops Rose Essential Oil

Lavender Vanilla Sea Salt Body Scrub

- 1 cup Fine Sea Salt
- ½ cup your Choice of Carrier Oil
- 15 drops Lavender Oil
- 2 tsp. Vanilla Extract

Citrus Sea Salt Body Scrub

- 1 cup Fine Sea Salt
- ½ cup your Choice of Carrier Oil
- 5 drops Orange Essential Oil
- 5 drops Lemon Essential Oil
- 5 drops Grapefruit Essential Oil

Vanilla Sea Salt Body Scrub

- 1 cup Fine Sea Salt
- ½ cup your Choice of Carrier Oil
- 3 tbsp. Vanilla Extract

Orange and Ginger Sea Salt Body Scrub

- 1 cup Fine Sea Salt
- ½ cup your Choice of Carrier Oil
- 10 drops Orange Essential Oil
- 5 drops Ginger Essential Oil

Lavender and Chamomile Sea Salt Body Scrub

- 1 cup Fine Sea Salt
- ½ cup your Choice of Carrier Oil
- 8 drops Lavender Essential Oil
- 8 drops Chamomile Essential Oil

Peppermint and Eucalyptus Sea Salt Body Scrub

- 1 cup Fine Sea Salt
- ½ cup your Choice of Carrier Oil
- 8 drops Peppermint Essential Oil

8 drops Eucalyptus Essential Oil

Conclusion

You now have all the knowledge you need to create DIY body scrubs at home. Explore the different combinations and find what works the best for your skin. Use the knowledge to pamper yourself. You could also pamper your friends and family by gifting them a jar of your homemade body scrub. Let them discover all the fantastic benefits of regular exfoliation. The possibilities are limitless. Enjoy the creative process as you journey to glowing, healthy skin.

References

Ballinger, K. (2018, October 17). Preservatives, shelf life & safety information. The Inspired Little Pot. https://theinspiredlittlepot.com.au/blog/preservatives-shelf-life-and-safety-information/

Borah, P. (2020, March 20). How to make coffee scrub at home for gorgeous skin. Swirlster.Ndtv.Com. https://swirlster.ndtv.com/beauty/how-to-make-coffee-scrub-at-home-for-gorgeous-skin-2202977

Brady, K. (2019a, January 25). 5 reasons dermatologists say you should rub grapeseed oil into your skin. Prevention. https://www.prevention.com/beauty/skin-care/a26038564/grapeseed-oil-skin-benefits/

Brady, K. (2019b, March 20). How to choose the best coconut oil for your skin and hair, according to dermatologists. Prevention. https://www.prevention.com/beauty/g26886381/best-coconut-oil/

Buddy Scrub. (n.d.). The benefits of jojoba oil. Retrieved October 2, 2020, from https://www.buddyscrub.com.au/blogs/news/52629443-the-benefits-of-jojoba-oil

Couic Marinier, Dr. F. (n.d.). Sweet orange - Essential oils for skincare. Www.Decleor.Com. Retrieved October 3, 2020, from https://www.decleor.com/en/oil-effects/melanin-inhibition/sweet-orange.html

Daniels, L. (2020, April 29). Almond oil for skin: Uses and research. Www.Medicalnewstoday.Com. https://www.medicalnewstoday.com/articles/almond-oil-for-skin

Derrick, J. (2020a, March 3). The right way to use a body scrub and a dry brush. Byrdie. https://www.byrdie.com/the-right-way-to-apply-a-body-scrub-345699

Derrick, J. (2020b, March 5). How to avoid ingrown hairs and razor burn, according to dermatologists. Byrdie. https://www.byrdie.com/top-shaving-tips-346378

Do, E. (2020, January 20). Do you use body scrub before or after soap? The right way. Be Young Aholic. https://beyoungaholic.com/do-you-use-body-scrub-before-or-after-soap/

Dresden, D. (2020, April 15). Is coconut oil good for your skin? Types and uses. Www.Medicalnewstoday.Com. https://www.medicalnewstoday.com/articles/coconut-oil-good-for-skin

Elliott, B. (2020, February 19). Top 6 benefits of taking collagen supplements. Healthline. https://www.healthline.com/nutrition/collagen-benefits

Essential oils and animals: Which essential oils are toxic for pets? (2018, March 22). Michelson Found Animals. https://www.foundanimals.org/essential-oils-toxic-pets/

Essential oils during pregnancy: What's safe and what to avoid. (2019, June 30). Parents. https://www.parents.com/pregnancy/my-body/pregnancy-health/essential-oils-during-pregnancy-whats-safe-and-what-to-avoid/

Essential oils that are more likely to cause irritation and skin sensitization. (n.d.). Aroma Web. Retrieved October 3, 2020, from https://www.aromaweb.com/articles/essential-oils-that-cause-irritation-sensitization.asp

Ferguson, S. (2019, July 15). DIY body scrubs: 5 easy recipes to exfoliate your skin. Healthline. https://www.healthline.com/health/skin/diy-body-scrub

References

Gallagher, G. (2019, September 30). Almond oil for your face: Benefits and how to use. Healthline. https://www.healthline.com/health/beauty-skin-care/almond-oil-for-face

Gerber, S. (2020, May 13). DIY basic homemade scrub formula (+ Endless variations!). Hello Glow. https://helloglow.co/homemade-body-scrub-formula/

Golan, T. L. (2017, June 2). The perfect guide: Homemade body scrub + my favorite body scrub recipe. Hedonisitit. https://www.hedonistit.com/perfect-guide-homemade-body-scrub-favorite-body-scrub-recipe/

Gotter, A. (2018, December 17). How to improve the health of your skin with lavender oil. Healthline. https://www.healthline.com/health/lavender-oil-for-skin

Groza, D. (2019, October 17). 10 DIY scrubs to make your skin glow. Hello Glow. https://helloglow.co/faves-10-diy-scrubs-make-skin-glow/

Hazardous essential oils. (n.d.). Aroma Web. Retrieved October 3, 2020, from https://www.aromaweb.com/essentialoils/hazardous.asp

Henry, E. (2018, August 14). Benefits of sugar scrubs for your skin. Suburban Simplicity. https://www.suburbansimplicity.com/benefits-sugar-scrubs

Herman, A., & Herman, A. P. (2013). Caffeine's mechanisms of action and its cosmetic use. Skin Pharmacology and Physiology, 26(1), 8–14. https://doi.org/10.1159/000343174

How to use body scrub. (2020, May 27). Thymes. https://www.thymes.com/Blog/How-To-Use-Body-Scrubs/

How to use body scrubs on your skin. (n.d.). Love Beauty and Planet. Retrieved September 30, 2020, from https://www.lovebeautyandplanet.com/us/en/the-love-beauty-planet-movement/our-purpose/our-blog/how-to-use-body-scrub-to-exfoliate.html

Jahns, E. (2019, September 23). Coconut oil for your skin: The complete guide. Byrdie. https://www.byrdie.com/coconut-oil-for-skin

Jones, E. (2020). 10 best essential oils for sugar scrubs & their reviews [Updated 2020]. Call Me Oil. https://callmeoil.com/best-essential-oil-for-sugar-scrubs/

Julia. (2019, December). Glow sugar scrub (DIY sugar body scrub). The Simple Veganista. https://simple-veganista.com/diy-edible-sugar-scrub/

Karen, S. (2017, December 20). Last minute sugar scrubs {How to make multiple scrubs with one recipe!}. No Fuss Natural. https://nofussnatural.com/last-minute-sugar-scrubs/

Kazan, S. (2018, December 17). DIY coconut oil sugar scrub recipe. Alphafoodie. https://www.alphafoodie.com/coconut-body-scrub/

Kimber, I., & Gerberick, F. G. (2007, December 6). Skin sensitization: What is it? Why is it important? What are the challenges? AltTox.Org. http://alttox.org/skin-sensitization-what-is-it-why-is-it-important-what-are-the-challenges/

Lapidos, R. (2019, May 1). Your A-Z guide to the antioxidants you need for your skin-care regimen. Well+Good. https://www.wellandgood.com/antioxidants-for-skin-benefits/

Mandy Zee. (2020, February 27). 9 essential benefits of peppermint oil. Byrdie. https://www.byrdie.com/benefits-of-peppermint-oil

McCabe, S. (2019, June 7). Brown sugar vs. white sugar: What's the difference? Healthline. https://www.healthline.com/nutrition/brown-sugar-vs-white-sugar#production

McCulloch, M. (2019, January 8). What is turbinado sugar? Nutrition, uses, and substitutes. Healthline. https://www.healthline.com/nutrition/turbinado-sugar#nutritiona

McEntee, K. (2020, June 29). Grapeseed oil is the beauty ingredient you didn't know you needed. Byrdie. https://www.byrdie.com/grape-seed-oil-beauty

Micah. (2017, June 14). 25 healing benefits of peppermint

oil. Alyaka. https://www.alyaka.com/magazine/25-healing-benefits-peppermint-oil/

Murphy, N. (2020, February 27). How to use almond oil for skin and get all the glowy benefits. Byrdie. https://www.byrdie.com/almond-oil-for-skin

Nordqvist, J. (2019, March 4). Lavender: Health benefits and uses. Medical News Today. https://www.medicalnewstoday.com/articles/265922

Ogee. (n.d.). Top 10 benefits of jojoba oil for skin. https://ogee.com/blogs/the-daily-good/top-10-benefits-of-jojoba-oil-for-skin

Pollard, S. (2020, April 30). Everything you need to know about making salt scrubs. Hello Glow. https://helloglow.co/salt-scrub/

Quinn, J., Articles, M., & March 23, 2018. (2018, March 23). Keeping your skin beautiful: Is exfoliation the anti-aging secret you need? Showbiz Cheat Sheet. https://www.cheatsheet.com/gear-style/exfoliation-anti-aging.html/

Rivas, G. (2020, May 1). Should you use a body scrub before or after body wash? Skincare.Com by L'Oréal. https://www.skincare.com/article/beauty-debate-when-to-use-body-scrub

Rud, M. (2020, March 12). Here's why jojoba oil is one of the most beloved skincare oils. Byrdie. https://www.byrdie.com/jojoba-oil-for-skin-4783234

Santos-Longhurst, A. (2018, October 22). Meaning of exfoliating: What is it, why you should, and how to start. Healthline. https://www.healthline.com/health/beauty-skin-care/meaning-of-exfoliating

Seladi-Schulman, J. (2019, October 3). Orange essential oil uses, benefits, and safety. Healthline. https://www.healthline.com/health/orange-essential-oil-uses

Should you exfoliate before or after shaving? (n.d.). Dove US. Retrieved October 1, 2020, from https://www.dove.-

com/us/en/stories/tips-and-how-to/washing-and-bathing-tips/should-you-exfoliate-before-or-after-shaving.html

Shunatona, B. (2020a, June 16). Not just for sleep: Here's how lavender oil can soothe and heal your skin. Byrdie. https://www.byrdie.com/lavender-oil-for-skin-4801192

Shunatona, B. (2020b, July 9). Okay, wait—Is coconut oil actually the key to perfect skin? Cosmopolitan. https://www.cosmopolitan.com/style-beauty/beauty/a27305882/coconut-oil-benefits-skin/

Sinha, R. (2018, September 17). 10 simple DIY coffee scrub recipes for smoother skin. Stylecraze. https://www.stylecraze.com/articles/diy-coffee-scrub-recipes-for-smoother-skin/

Smith-Garcia, D. (2020, May 19). Essential oils for pregnancy: What's safe and what to avoid. Healthline. https://www.healthline.com/health/pregnancy/essential-oils-for-pregnancy

Stanborough, R. J. (2019, August 9). The benefits of rose oil and how to use it. Healthline. https://www.healthline.com/health/rose-oil#1

Surian, A. (2012, October 15). Homemade sugar scrub. Happy Hour Projects. https://happyhourprojects.com/homemade-sugar-scrub/

Sweeney, M. (2020, August 20). Do essential oils expire? Average shelf life and how to extend. Healthline. https://www.healthline.com/health/do-essential-oils-expire

The Benefits of Jojoba Oil | Nourished Life. (2017, January 23). Nourished Life. https://www.nourishedlife.com.au/article/146099/benefits-of-jojoba-oil.html

The health and beauty benefits of a body scrub. (2016, September 17). Canyon Ranch. https://www.canyonranch.com/blog/beauty/the-health-and-beauty-benefits-of-a-body-scrub/

The importance of exfoliating your body. (2018, August

20). Cocokind. https://www.cocokind.com/blogs/news/exfoliating-your-body

Tiffinay. (2018, April 12). Coffee Body scrub with coconut oil. The Coconut Mama. https://thecoconutmama.com/coffee-body-scrub/

Watson, A. (2019, August 23). Sweet almond oil: What it is, what it does. Camille Beckman. https://camillebeckman.com/blogs/vie-de-camille/sweet-almond-oil-what-it-is-what-it-does

Watson, K. (2019, October 3). Grapeseed oil for skin. Healthline. https://www.healthline.com/health/grapeseed-oil-for-skin

Whitley, A. (2020, June 11). The importance and benefits of skin exfoliation. Truly Scrumptious Beauty. https://tsbeauty.co.uk/articles/skincare/benefits-skin-exfoliation/

Williams, B. (n.d.). How to store homemade sugar body scrub. LEAFtv. Retrieved October 4, 2020, from https://www.leaf.tv/articles/how-to-store-homemade-sugar-body-scrub/

Wilson, D. R. (2018, August 7). Coffee benefits for skin: Cellulite, brightening, anti-aging, and more. Healthline. https://www.healthline.com/health/coffee-benefits-for-skin#benefits

Wong, C. (2016). The health benefits of lavender essential oil. Verywell Mind. https://www.verywellmind.com/lavender-for-less-anxiety-3571767

Wong, C. (2020, August 27). Health benefits of rose essential oil. Verywell Health. https://www.verywellhealth.com/the-benefits-of-rose-essential-oil-88790

About the Author

Monique Joiner Siedlak is a writer, witch, and warrior on a mission to awaken people to their greatest potential through the power of storytelling infused with mysticism, modern paganism, and new age spirituality. At the young age of 12, she began rigorously studying the fascinating philosophy of Wicca. By the time she was 20, she was self-initiated into the craft, and hasn't looked back ever since. To this day, she has authored over 40 books pertaining to the magick and mysteries of life.

To find out more about Monique Joiner Siedlak artistically, spiritually, and personally, feel free to visit her **official website**.

www.mojosiedlak.com

f facebook.com/mojosiedlak

𝕏 twitter.com/mojosiedlak

⊙ instagram.com/mojosiedlak

⊕ pinterest.com/mojosiedlak

BB bookbub.com/authors/monique-joiner-siedlak

Other Books by Author

African Magic

Hoodoo

Seven African Powers: The Orishas

Cooking For the Orishas

Lucumi: The Ways of Santeria

Voodoo of Louisiana

Practical Magick

Wiccan Basics

Candle Magick

Wiccan Spells

Love Spells

Abundance Spells

Herb Magick

Moon Magick

Creating Your Own Spells

Gypsy Magic

Personal and Self Development

Astral Projection for Beginners

Meditation for Beginners

Reiki for Beginners

Manifesting With the Law of Attraction

Stress Management

Time Bound: Setting Your Goals

Healing Animals with Reiki

The Yoga Collective

Yoga for Beginners

Yoga for Stress

Yoga for Back Pain

Yoga for Weight Loss

Yoga for Flexibility

Yoga for Advanced Beginners

Yoga for Fitness

Yoga for Runners

Yoga for Energy

Yoga for Your Sex Life

Yoga to Beat Depression and Anxiety

Yoga for Menstruation

Yoga to Detox Your Body

Toga to Tone Your Body

Last Chance
Join My Newsletter!

If you missed it, I have a free gift available for you and wanted to remind you it's still available.

mojosiedlak.com/self-help-and-yoga-newsletter

Thank you for reading my book.
I really appreciate all your feedback and would love to hear what you have to say!
Please leave your review at your favorite retailer!

www.ingramcontent.com/pod-product-compliance
Lightning Source LLC
Chambersburg PA
CBHW071638040426
42452CB00009B/1690